FAITH
RULES
AN EPISCOPAL MANUAL

IAN S. MARKHAM
WITH SAMANTHA R. E. GOTTLICH

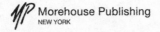

Morehouse Publishing
NEW YORK

For our mothers, who always had faith in us:

Beryl Evelyn Markham
(1927–1981)

Jennifer Rose Gottlich
(1957–2015)

Copyright © 2016 by Ian S. Markham

Unless otherwise noted, the Scripture quotations contained herein are from the New Revised Standard Version Bible, copyright © 1989 by the Division of Christian Education of the National Council of Churches of Christ in the U.S.A. Used by permission. All rights reserved.

Morehouse Publishing, 19 East 34th Street, New York, NY 10016

Morehouse Publishing is an imprint of Church Publishing Incorporated.
www.churchpublishing.org

Cover design by Jennifer Kopec, 2Pug Design
Typeset by Rose Design

Library of Congress Cataloging-in-Publication Data

A record of this book is available from the Library of Congress

ISBN-13: 978-0-8192-3297-7 (pbk.)
ISBN-13: 978-0-8192-3298-4 (ebook)

Printed in the United States of America

Contents

Foreword

The truth is that none of us have ever lived before. From the youngest infant to the oldest elder we are all novices, kindergarteners, beginners at life.

I suspect that is one reason we need God. If I may say it this way, God has been around quite a while. The Bible sometimes speaks of God as "Ancient of Days." There is a great well of wisdom for living in the Divine. And the human family has also learned some things over time, well worth passing on.

Ian Markham and Samantha Gottlich are two disciples of Jesus, yet two people representing different generations, two people from different countries of birth, one the dean of a seminary and the other seminarian studying at a seminary.

They share two profoundly significant bonds, though. They are both children of God, and they are both baptized disciples of Jesus Christ.

A disciple is one who learns from and lives by the teaching and wisdom of a great teacher. We who are Christian are disciples of Jesus of Nazareth, learners of his way, living in his Spirit.

In this wonderful book, or guidebook, or tract for our times, they have gathered and given voice to some rules of faith and living that have roots ancient and deep. The wisdom in these pages has been gathered over the centuries of human beings living in relationship with the God and with fellow human beings. What they share with us here is nothing less than the wisdom of the Way of Jesus, the wisdom of the Ancient of days who came among us in the person, the life, and the teachings of Jesus of Nazareth.

In one of their rules they suggest that the great composers know that the miracle of music is really the result of the mystical discovery of the transcendent in our midst. And that mysterious process of creation by a composer can lift the hearer up into the same transcendent realm of glory when the music is played or performed.

But part of the mystery of the miracle is that the music is made by reading and interpreting little notes on a piece of paper.

This book is a series of little notes. But what music they make.

—Yours in Christ,
✠ Michael B. Curry
Presiding Bishop of The Episcopal Church

Acknowledgments

"**R**ead this," Davis Perkins, the publisher of Church Publishing Inc., said to me as we sat together having a Coke at General Convention in Salt Lake City. It was Michael Pollan's *Food Rules*. "And think about the question: what would The Episcopal Church equivalent look like?" he added. On the flight home, I did so. It was a great read—one epigram on each page, with a short explanation. The epigrams were memorable, wise, and insightful. By the end of the flight, I had a draft of sixty-four rules for *Faith Rules*.

Therefore let me begin by expressing my gratitude to Davis Perkins. He is a hardworking, proactive publisher who is constantly ready to work with an author to fill a gap that the market doesn't yet know is there. It is impressive. It is always a delight to work with him.

Robert Heaney suggested the title; Samantha Gottlich brought excitement, energy, and a willingness to draft rules. We convened a small group of readers; so thank you to Dr. Lisa Kimball, Ms. Heather Zdancewicz, Ms. Jackie Bray, Mr. Austin Smith, Mr. Luke Markham, and my wife, Lesley Markham. Naturally all mistakes remain our responsibility, but we appreciated the energy and advice.

Wendell Berry gave us permission to reproduce his poem, "Grace," from *Poetry Magazine*, June 1967. We are grateful to Ryan Masteller for his careful stewardship of the manuscript into production and to the highly talented Benjamin Hart who has produced the remarkable illustrations.

Finally, writing is always a shared role. Katherine Malloy in my office creates the space in the calendar. My senior team—Melody Knowles, Barney Hawkins, Heather Zdancewicz, Katie Glover, and Justin Lewis-Anthony—are a great support at all times. And as the book was written, I appreciated afresh our friendship with Gloria Ventura.

—Ian Markham

◆ ◆ ◆

I share Ian's gratitude to Davis Perkins and to the team who read our manuscript. Thank you for supporting us in this project. And I am grateful to Ian for the opportunity to collaborate on this book. It has been a great experience.

Writing this book has offered me time to reflect on my own faith journey, so I'd like to take this opportunity to thank all those who started and helped me along the way. To my grandparents, who gave me my first Bible and introduced me to The Episcopal Church, the countless youth leaders, camp counselors, and priests who showed me what it meant to live and love in Christian community, and my brother, JD, for being the love project incarnate, thank you. I'm especially grateful to my students, co-workers, and mentors at the Episcopal Student Center at the University of Texas who lifted me up and affirmed my calling throughout the discernment process for Holy Orders. I'm grateful to Austin Smith for the courage, strength, and faith he shares with me every day. And I am thankful for the faithful guidance and mentorship I continually find within my community at Virginia Theological Seminary.

—SAMANTHA GOTTLICH

Introduction

Faith Rules is an invitation to live life under the rule of faith, through these sixty-seven rules that take a person to faith and then into the Christian faith and then into The Episcopal Church. It is written out of the conviction that life lived in the context of faith is the only way to live authentically. We believe that God really is. We believe that if we live attuned to the deep dynamics of existence, then we will sense the transcendent love of the cosmic all around us. Therefore we start the book with an invitation to the seeker to start living life sensitive to the depth and textured nature of reality.

This book is written out of the sense that the tradition of Anglicanism, which is embodied in the form of the Episcopal Church here in the United States, is a beautiful blend of thoughtfulness and faithfulness that can speak powerfully to the predicaments and challenges of being human in the twenty-first century. Religion is often ugly. It can be intolerant, bigoted, cruel, anti-intellectual, and unable to accommodate modern discoveries. The Episcopal Church tries very hard to witness to an alternative reading of faith. We aspire to learn from and accommodate the best of modernity; we welcome disagreement; we want to challenge our deep-seated prejudices; we believe that reason has an important role to play in faith; and we try as hard as we can to focus on the big picture, what we are calling "the love project." **The Love Project is the goal of creation: God created this universe so we might learn how to give and receive love.** This is what faith is all about. Now, we are not the only tradition doing this, but we are one of the traditions that does this, so this book is an invitation to discover The Episcopal Church.

Religion is a deadly serious topic. People are willing to kill over religion. And it is vast and complicated. So our other goal in this book is to capture a lightness of touch. We want the text to be accessible to someone who is completely unfamiliar with, or distrustful of, religion. Inevitably, this means that complexities are ruthlessly simplified and sometimes nuance is lost. We felt that we had no choice but to do this. Accessibility had to trump detail. Right at the end of the book, you will find suggestions for follow-up and additional reading. This book is intended to be the start of a journey, not the end of one.

Finally, the book can be read in a variety of ways. One could read it all in one sitting; one could read a section at a time; one could even read a rule at a time. Once read, we hope it is a book you will return to as you learn afresh about life lived authentically in the context of the transcendent.

—Ian S. Markham and Samantha R. E. Gottlich

Section One

RULES FOR FINDING FAITH

To appreciate experiences, you need a guide. Appreciating architectural genius requires a guide who explains to you the differences between brickwork that is flemish bond (alternating stretchers—which is where bricks are placed long side—and headers—which is where bricks are placed short side) and basket weave (where pairs of bricks are laid vertically and then another pair horizontally). In fact, you don't notice the differences in brickwork until someone points this out to you. Appreciating the nose (the smell) on a glass of wine requires a person who can invite you to find grass cuttings and gooseberries in a Sauvignon Blanc or the blackcurrants in a glass of red Zinfandel. Appreciating the achievement of football requires a guide who can explain the blitz, zone read, and fumble. Without these guides, we just don't see the depth and texture of life. Without the guide, bricks are just bricks; wine is just wine; and football is just football. We stop at the surface and don't dig deeper.

In the first six rules, you will find an invitation to see the normal and mundane in a new and different way. It is an invitation to look beyond the surface experience of life to see depth and texture. Look hard enough and you will start to see the transcendent and the spiritual all around you.

Disconnect from the tech

Most of us live with our heads stuck in the immediate. Our senses are bombarded by sounds and sights generated by screens. We are plugged in—listening to music or a podcast or audiobook; we are sliding our hands over a phone to read the latest text, e-mail, and Facebook status update; and we are moving from a laptop to a tablet to a smartphone constantly. Never is there a moment when we are not connected.

So let us start by putting all this stuff down. Let us disconnect from our virtual world and engage with the real world. Pause and focus for a moment on the moment. Find the quietest place you can and listen attentively to the silence. Hear how interesting and deep the silence is. The great spiritual guides of humanity invite us to become conscious of our bodies—focus especially on the miracle of breath. Feel the action of inhaling, followed by the action of exhaling. Move around your body inviting each part to relax. Do this by tensing an area, for example, your feet and ankles, and then instruct the area to relax. Move from your feet up to your waist, right up to your shoulders and head. Marvel at the complex story that science tells about our bodies. Notice the miracle of yourself.

This is basic meditation; it is what the Buddhists would call "mindfulness." Mindfulness is an awareness of the moment and everything that is going on inside you; it is entering deep inside, while making no judgments and acknowledging the feelings, thoughts, and bodily sensations. If you go no further in this book, then this basic practice is worth learning. The health benefits of mindfulness are considerable.

But we want you to notice something more. We want you to allow the silence to embrace you. Allow yourself to marvel at who you are. And at a stroke, you have started the journey to faith. The embrace of silence is the presence of God surrounding you; the miracle of you is the gift of being made possible by God. Welcome to the journey of faith.

2

Walk, linger, and marvel

We are always going somewhere. The journey is often a means to an end. For most of us the journey is a drive. If we walk at all, then it consists of the stroll to a car to then be transported from home to wherever—the grocery store. This rule invites us to walk with no regard for the destination. Find a park, maybe a river, perhaps just an interesting street—and walk slowly, pausing to admire the grass that peeks through a crack in the sidewalk, or the tree that was there a long time before you were born, or the bird chirping on the edge of a wall. Everywhere you look there are wonders of life abounding.

The story of life is amazing. Through an elaborate process of natural selection the biodiversity of the world came to be. Life is a journey of 3.8 billion years. Just take that in. The faith instinct sees life as intended. God's chosen mechanism was evolution. Everything has purpose.

Seeing the world around us as intended is an act of faith. We are taking the risk of seeing things differently. Pause and marvel—suddenly, we matter.

3

Enjoy the company of someone you love

Solitude and silence are packed with signs of the transcendent; they make you aware that you are part of a bigger picture—that living is part of a bigger story that comes from above and surrounds us. But so is company. Now you need to find someone you can love—a friend, spouse, child, parent, or sibling. Enter into a conversation where you explore the other. Every person is a deep well of complexity. So explore this person you love—remember together, laugh together, and discover together.

So what is love? Is it just a trick of the evolutionary process to encourage parents to care for their young or spouses to reproduce? Or is it more? Reflect on the rich conversations you have had with the one you love. Think about the feelings deep inside of you that you have for the special one. The Christian claim is that love is our purpose for being; it is the reason the world was made. The God, which is goodness and love at the heart of the universe enabling everything that is and sustaining everything that is, invites us to discover love. We are created out of love in order to love. We are hardwired for connection with others. The love two people share is a glimpse of our divinely intended purpose for being.

4

Let the music take you higher

What do Bach, Beethoven, Handel, Haydn, Liszt, and Rachmaninoff all have in common? What do Bono, Faith Hill, Kristin Chenoweth, and the Jonas Brothers all have in common? The answer is not simply that they were amazing composers, but also that they were persons of faith. It was George Steiner who observed that great musicians have an heightened sensitivity to the transcendent; very few are atheists. They really believe that their music is a discovery; there are certain notes that are just right for the piece that they are seeking to birth. And of course, as we listen to great music, we cannot help being lifted out of ourselves into the realm of the transcendent. As one closes one's eyes, the music does indeed take you higher.

And all of this is made possible by the simple notations on a page. A musical score looks so flat upon the page. Yet when these notations are taken, interpreted, and voiced, out from the page comes forth music that resonates with the chords of our souls. Music has power. Music can capture our feelings for us (think how often it is music that helps us get over a relationship breakup); music can aid recollection (think how often we listen to that old childhood song that instantly brings to mind where we were and what we were doing); and music can cut to our very souls (those moments when the music is all we are hearing).

Music is a glimpse into the divine. It is a gateway; it is a vehicle into the transcendent.

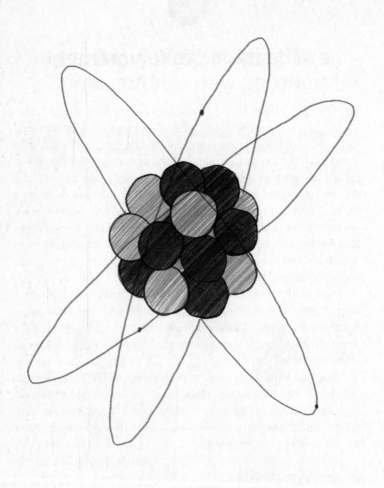

5

Recognize that we are infinitely more than just complex bundles of atoms that came from nowhere and go nowhere

Faith is the act of seeing the world in a certain way. It is the capacity to see that life is not just the immediate, the ephemeral, but it is much more. Life has texture; life has depth. How do we make sense of this depth? One option is the answer of reductionist science. Everything is made up of complex bundles of atoms that come from nowhere and ultimately go nowhere. There are many problems with this. Quantum mechanics talks about a universe that is much more mysterious and puzzling. At the quantum level, there is unpredictability and openness. But more, reductionist science just feels wrong. Love is not just a trick of the evolutionary process to encourage us to reproduce. Music is not just a remarkable human achievement. Mind is not just reducible to brain activity. Life's depth and texture point to something more than that; they point toward the transcendent.

Faith affirms we are in an intended universe. We are meant to be here. The Goodness and Love at the heart of the universe wanted humanity to emerge. The response of faith need not conflict with the insights we are learning from science. Antibiotics work and, when you have an infection, are great. Evolution is true; the multiverse might be true. Truths learned through science are part of the picture. But we locate our scientific picture of the world within a bigger framework of the transcendent. One that we correctly intuit (or sense) is part of the truth about reality.

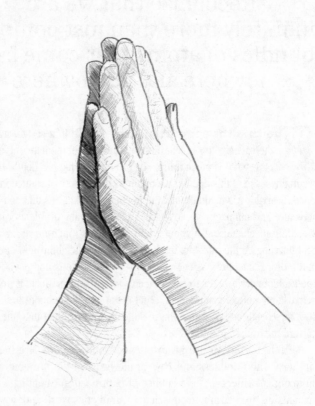

6

Allow yourself to pray

Prayer is the connection of the soul with the transcendent (the height and depth of everything) that is all around us. The soul is our fundamental self; it is our core being and identity. Prayer happens when we open our inner being to conversation—to communion—with the loving embrace of the transcendent. Prayers sometimes use words, but, perhaps, more often do not. In fact, it might feel quite strange to speak with words at first. Therefore, especially at its core, prayer is the act of enjoying quiet, becoming conscious of the fact that we are loved, and allowing that love to surround us.

Prayer is felt and experienced. Thinking too much is unhelpful. Put aside your pictures of God and suspend your questions for a moment. Instead just allow the desire for love to come forth from your soul. This can be either verbal or silent. And then allow yourself to sense that God's love is present, real, and surrounding you.

The first conscious prayer is the baby step of faith. It is the act of relocating our lives away from the mundane and immediate and into the real and transcendent. Now we are living our lives on multiple levels—both in the immediate moment and the deeper more textured level of the transcendent. Welcome to the world of faith.

Section Two

RULES FOR ALL YOUR CHOICES AND HOW TO MAKE ONE

So you have arrived at faith, but how do you decide which religion is right? This looks like a massive problem. But actually if you think about any other subject, this problem is much less significant. Economists divide into monetarists and Keynesians (as well as many other groups); psychologists divide into Jungians and Freudians (and many other groups). Disagreement in these subjects is not evidence for the non-existence of the economy or the non-existence of the psyche. Instead, we recognize that disagreement is inevitable because of the complexity of these areas. What is true in economics and psychology is even more true in religion. **Metaphysics** (i.e. the study of ultimate reality) is especially complicated. Fortunately, we have been thinking about religion for several millennia, so the collective wisdom of the world in this area is amazing. And there are certain insights that the major religions agree on. Most agree that the transcendent is best spoken about as an underlying unity (ultimately there is the oneness underpinning everything) and that we are being invited into a life-transforming project of love. Religious diversity, then, isn't a threat to faith.

But on what basis do we decide to follow Jesus? What we have to do is encounter the living Son of God we find in the church and in the Bible. We will suggest that the **Gospels** (the books in the Bible about Jesus' life and teachings) "have the ring of truth" (to use J.B. Phillips's lovely phrase). We are invited to make the decision to follow Jesus as an act of trust grounded in the plausibility of the witness of the Gospels.

7

Remember it is all about the love project

So what is this love project? When people ask the question, "Why did God create the universe?," the answer of the major religions is that God created the universe as the setting in which women and men can learn the hard work of giving and receiving love. This is God's project. This is the love project.

Religious people are often the strongest argument for atheism. We can be so unkind and cruel. Points of principle (often of a pretty abstract form) become reasons for schism. We have a long list of folks we dislike, which often includes all the adherents of the other religions. In the past, we wrote lengthy tracts defending patriarchy and slavery. We can be smug, indifferent, and downright unpleasant.

It is worth remembering that our core experience of God is of a unity that surrounds us with love. The primary theme underpinning the message of countless prophets, teachers, and priests is that the divine calls us to focus less on ourselves and more on others. The big picture here is really important. Any religious community that is not life-enhancing and does not lead to the goals of peace and love is wrong. You must stay away from it.

Now being in a community that is focused on the life-enhancing love project is not easy. It is hard. One of the reasons religious people can be so unpleasant is that they are human. And people everywhere have moments when they enjoy being selfish, tribal, unkind, and even cruel. Sitting around in a like-minded group and complaining about Democrats, Republicans, immigrants, Muslims, liberal elites, or the homophobic Westboro Baptist Church is great fun. So don't be misled: focusing on the love project is hard work and challenging. Do know, however, that it is worth all the struggle, challenge, and hard work. A life focused on self is tragic and lonely; a life focused on love is rewarding and enhancing.

8

God is complex—so don't be surprised that folks understand God in different ways

Surprise! God is complicated. Religion is in the business of talking about ultimate reality. The disciplines of economics and physics are complicated. But religion is even bigger; it embraces economics, physics, and every other subject. Religion is an attempt to describe the origins and nature of the author and designer of this cosmos (and if there are other universes—those as well).

Now with any complicated topic there are many vantage points. Different cultures generated different accounts of ultimate reality. This happened in every subject—the science of Aristotle is different from ancient Han Chinese science, which in turn is different from the science of Newton. Different economic models emerged in different cultures over time from the very simple—the hunting and gathering economic model of certain tribes—to the very complicated, like capitalism or planned economies.

The point is different cultures in different times arrived at different accounts of everything, from science to economics to religion. It is just the way the knowing process works. We live in community and strive to make sense of our complicated experience of life. As we do so, different theories and traditions emerge in different places.

9

Don't believe God is a robot—do believe God is Spirit

I t is possible to decide between different accounts of God. Some are more plausible than others. Some are more coherent than others. We use our reason. Self-contradictory accounts of God are unlikely to be true (God cannot be both within time and timeless); some accounts have an elegant simplicity (so one God is more likely to be true than a whole pantheon of gods all squabbling together); and some make sense of key themes both of the world Scriptures and our experience (so every tradition that believes in God postulates a God that is calling us to live according to transcendent moral standards).

The weird thing is that if you take the four influential religions—Hinduism, Judaism, Christianity, and Islam—there is agreement about the basics. God is a unity—the oneness of God; God is creator; God is a revealing God—telling us in a variety of ways what God is like; and God is love—inviting us all into the love project.

Naturally there are differences between the religions, for example, the nature of the afterlife. However, on the big picture, there is agreement.

Trust that God has spoken in Jesus

All religions trust that somewhere God has spoken. For the Hindus, it is the Upanishads; for Jews, the Torah; and for Muslims, the Qur'an. So Christians believe that the definitive disclosure of God is a life. Christians believe that Jesus Christ (the Jew who lived approximately two thousand years ago in Israel) is the very utterance of God on earth. In other words, when you look at that life you see what God is like. To use traditional language, Jesus is the Eternal Word made flesh.

Feel free to look and learn about all the world's religions. And in the process take a long look at Jesus. In the very words and deeds of Jesus of Nazareth, Christians believe we can see God. In the words of Jesus, we learn of a God that is constantly calling us to be better than we are—to really live holy and loving lives. In the deeds of Jesus, we learn that God doesn't give up on anyone (we know that from the company that Jesus kept). As you learn about Jesus it's possible to fall in love with Jesus.

In the end, deciding to follow Jesus is an act of trust. It is grounded in what we learn about Jesus from the Gospels and then the impact of Jesus on our lives through the people of God, the church.

Read the Bible—start with the Gospels

OK, now you need to start reading the Bible. And you start with the Gospels because they are all about Jesus—the Eternal Word made flesh.

The Gospels tell the stories of Jesus Christ, God's **incarnation** (i.e. God was uniquely present and identical with the human Jesus) in the world. As you trust that God has spoken in Jesus, read about his life. Let the Gospels offer you a way to learn about the complexities of a man fully human and fully divine. Journey through the miracle of his birth, the gathering and teaching of his disciples, his miraculous works and his earnest love for the world. Read about his suffering, the sting of death that encompasses him, and the mysterious awe that awakens in his Resurrection.

There are four Gospels. Each of them offers threads of familiarity in the life of Jesus, but each of them also offers a unique perspective that allows us to discover a fuller, more holistic vision of Jesus and God's revelation in him. Experience the urgency of Mark, the teachings and authority of Matthew, the praise and challenge of Luke, and the divine mysteries and wisdom of John. Allow them to paint the layers of Jesus's self onto a single canvas as you discover Jesus's identity and meaning in the life of the world.

Read the rest of the Bible

Don't let the size discourage you; it is a big book. The Bible is rich with history and story. And you have the rest of your life to discover the hidden gems in the corners of each of its pages. But you need to start, and you need to start now. Ease into the Bible. Perhaps start with 1 Corinthians 13, followed by the love poem the "Song

of Songs," then try the first eleven chapters of Genesis. Do not start at the beginning and just plough through: you will stop reading in the middle of Leviticus. Move around, reading some New Testament and then Old Testament in manageable portions. There are many different translations of the Bible. It was written long before the English language existed. We recommend the New Revised Standard Version because it is both a good translation from the Greek and Hebrew and readable English. However, if you are really coming to the Bible for the first time, then the New Living Translation is gender-inclusive and great fun.

These are the stories of our ancestors, the stories of our beginnings, the stories of our deep debt to Judaism, and the stories of our Christian inheritance. And it is actually quite a thrilling collection of books. Sixty-six books for us Episcopalians, more for our Roman Catholic friends. Now working through sixty-six books is hard work, but don't worry; if you've followed Rule 11, you've already read four! There is so much depth and breadth to the Bible. Are you struggling with life's sufferings? Give Job a read. Are you overjoyed with gratitude for the people in your life? Peruse Philippians. Do you sometimes wonder why Christianity is called an Abrahamic faith? Genesis is the book for you. And when you come across confusing or challenging names, events, or passages, read ahead to Rule 53. It's OK to struggle with the Bible.

Within the Bible we find our tradition, our heritage, our foundation as a people of God and as the followers of Jesus. Each reading can offer new meaning and connection in the context of your life. Find solace, comfort, hope, joy, and above all love within the pages of the Bible. Feel the roots of your life find grounding in the sands of Jerusalem and Galilee. Feel the connections of believers who have come before you and who will read these same pages long after you and know that this is our communal story to read, to share, and to live.

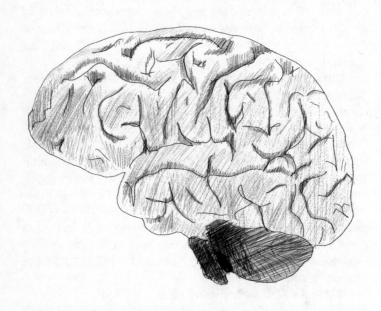

13

God gave us a mind so don't be afraid to use it

Faith is not blind. Faith is not irrational. Reason and faith are not opposites. In fact, St. Thomas Aquinas, the thirteenth-century Dominican friar, insisted that faith is built on reason. Plenty of our atheist friends think faith is believing despite the lack of evidence. It is not. Instead, Christians believe that our minds are God-given gifts. We should think about our faith. There are lively debates in Christianity about the best way to describe the **Trinity** or the nature of the afterlife. You are not required to believe stupid and implausible things; it is OK to think that Joshua did not stop the sun moving (Josh. 10) just to enable himself to have a few more daylight hours to kill the Amorites.

We trust that God has spoken in Jesus; we read the Bible carefully; we give a vote to all those who have come before; and yes we use our minds to evaluate the things we are learning. This is how God wants us to operate.

When Jesus is asked which is the most important commandment that God gave the Jewish people, Jesus replied: "Love the Lord your God with all your heart, and with all your soul, and with all your strength, and with all your mind" (Luke 10:27). We are commanded to love God with all our minds. That means thinking about our faith, discovering and embodying it intellectually as well as emotionally and spiritually.

Give a vote to those who came before you

So a picture is emerging. We trust that God has spoken in Jesus. We see the Word of God in a life. We learn of that life from the Bible. And now we locate the interpretation of that life in the journey of the church over two thousand years. G. K. Chesterton wrote, "Tradition means giving a vote to the most obscure of all classes, our ancestors. It is the democracy of the dead."[1] We need to listen to the past. Our Christian ancestors worked hard to make sense of what God was saying in Jesus. It is important to give appropriate weight to the seven ecumenical councils (from the Council of Nicaea in 325 CE to the seventh council, also in Nicaea, in 787 CE) when the Church agreed on some of the basics about God. We need to celebrate and learn from the wisdom of the saints who have gone before. Read a good introduction to the church fathers (look at the annotated bibliography at the end of this book). Marvel at the way they shaped the story of Christianity.

---

1. G. K. Chesterton, *Orthodoxy* (Nashville: Thomas Nelson, 2007), 207.

15

Add two years on to your life—go to church

It drives our secular friends crazy. But yes, actually going to church is really beneficial to your health. You will live longer. The precise reasons are puzzling. The social network probably helps. Loneliness is a crippling disease for many people; and once you are inside a church family, you always have someone to call. Perhaps church members are less likely to be involved in destructive behaviors, which might be a factor. But the evidence suggests that there are other things going on.

The weird thing is that you must actually go. You must get up on a Sunday morning, slip into some clothes, and go and stand with others in a congregation. Believing this stuff from a Starbucks or on the golf course or while reading *The New York Times* in your bathrobe isn't sufficient. You don't get the health benefits. It is the actual participation in a worshipping community that makes you healthier.

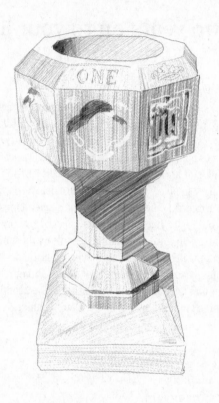

16

Get baptized

Getting wet in the middle of a service might seem to be a pretty stupid thing to do. However, rituals are powerful actions in which the symbolism is transforming. In the ritual of **baptism**, a person joins the Christian community.

One of the central themes of the Christian story is that God wants to transform us so that we can transform the world. The world is so often marked with death and destruction. As we choose to surrender our lives to God, as we choose to be washed by the waters of baptism, we are choosing to participate in the renewal of life. We are being made new, we are being transformed. And that transformation brings us into irrevocable relationship with God.

It might be helpful to spend some time in Scripture reading about baptism. Look to Matthew 3:13–17 for an account of Jesus' own baptism, Matthew 28:18–20 for the call for disciples to continue baptizing, and Colossians 2:11–12 and Romans 6:3–4 for a bigger picture of what our own baptisms mean. Engage in conversation with other Christians about it. Talk to a priest or pastor. Then, it is time to make a decision. Committing yourself to the Christian faith in baptism can be a monumentally challenging choice, but it will be the most transformative choice you ever make.

Give The Episcopal Church
a chance

In most towns across America there is an Episcopal Church. It may not be the largest. The Baptist Church and the Roman Catholic Church are larger. It will likely have a faded "The Episcopal Church Welcomes You" sign. There will probably be two services indicated on the sign—8 am Rite 1, 10 am Rite 2. It will be a traditional-looking church—perhaps with a steeple and an interior worship space designed in a cruciform shape (i.e. shaped like a cross). And yes we want you to give this church a go.

The first sixteen rules come out of the Episcopal tradition. If Baptists or Roman Catholics were writing this book, then there would be a different emphasis. The Episcopal niche is that we are faithful and thoughtful—we are traditional with our emphasis on **liturgy** (it is like following a script in a play) and the Bible, yet at the same time we recognize everyone is on a journey and we are not all in the same place. It is a wonderful balance of communal and individual focus.

Don't give up—The Episcopal Church really does welcome you!

Going to the first meeting of anything is tricky. Think of the number of times you have gone to a party with a friend and as your friend skips around talking to everyone, you gravitate alone to the food table or lean against the wall and people-watch. Folks hang out with the people they know; getting to know the stranger is hard work.

One further problem The Episcopal Church has with welcome is that we are never sure. We are not sure whether you are a newcomer or just a very intermittent attender. The Episcopal Church has lots of members who rarely come. Giving a warm newcomer's welcome to a person who has been a member for the last three decades is not good—they get upset. So you might want to try The Episcopal Church, but perhaps you are not sure how to engage.

So please take full advantage of the **peace.** The priest will say, "The peace of the Lord be always with you"; and the people reply, "and also with you." And then you will exchange the peace. Grab the hands of everyone around you. Take the opportunity to introduce yourself. Let people know you are new.

One thing we do not do is ask you to stand up in the middle of the service or slap the VISITOR sticker on your chest. We will not embarrass you; you are allowed to watch, observe, and think about whether this community can be home.

However, one warning: it is possible that apart from the peace, you were totally ignored. We are sorry about that. Please give The Episcopal Church another go. We really do welcome you and want you to find your spiritual home here. The clergy person will want to meet you. Please mention to the usher who gives you the bulletin that you are new and have never been to The Episcopal Church before. Ask if you can sit next to someone who can help you navigate the service (there are moments when it gets crazy—where exactly is S119?).

After a couple of times, the congregation will get it. And you really will feel welcome.

Section Three

RULES FOR BECOMING AN EPISCOPALIAN

Doing anything for the first time is strange. Going to your first concert is weird—you have to find the right door, learn when to cheer and clap, and when to stand up and sit down. Going to your first college basketball game is unusual—you have to learn the rules and convention (for UConn basketball games the crowd doesn't sit down until the first basket has been scored by UConn). The first few times it is just plain weird; to start with one is an observer, it is only later than one becomes a fan of the band or a supporter of the team.

We all push through the weirdness when it comes to concerts and sporting events, so we need to push through the weirdness of church. So here are nine rules to help you push past that initial stage where it is all strange and get to the place where you are less of an observer and more of a worshipper.

These rules apply to the basic liturgy that the vast majority of congregations provide on a Sunday morning. It is the Rite 2 (the modern language one) **Eucharist** (which means the bread and wine will be available). For other services, the rules would need some adapting.

19

Learn to juggle at least two books and do pew aerobics

Welcome to The Episcopal Church, where we have been training jugglers and aerobics instructors of all ages for centuries! OK—maybe that's a bit of a stretch—but we do get pretty proficient at holding, marking, switching, and juggling our two

main worship service resources: The **Book of Common Prayer** and The Hymnal. And we do get more exercise than the average churchgoer on a Sunday thanks to our beloved pew aerobics: we sit, stand, kneel, bow, and a whole host of other actions throughout a typical service.

The Book of Common Prayer is our service guide. It is comprised mostly of extracts from the Bible and lays out our order of worship, prayers, and psalms for the daily readings. You'll find both modern and traditional language, rites for Sunday services, funerals, marriages, baptisms and other events in the life of the church, and the **creeds** (our statements of faith) upon which we stand. It is a beautifully crafted guide to our church community.

The Hymnal is the other book you'll need on a regular basis. It is full of a whole host of musical pieces composed throughout history. We sing many times during a Sunday service, so it is helpful to keep it close at hand throughout your time in the pews. Our services are sometimes supplemented with other worship resources both for orders of worship and for music, but all of these supplemental books will be a breeze once you learn to juggle your first two. And even better, many churches are moving toward an all inclusive worship bulletin for each service so that we can focus less on juggling and more on worshipping.

The last thing to remember are the pew cues: we generally kneel or stand to pray, sit to listen, and stand to sing. There are exceptions to that, but just know that we like to pray with our bodies as well as our hearts, and sitting, standing, and kneeling are all ways to incorporate our whole selves into our worship.

One last thing, don't be surprised if half of the congregation does one thing and the other does something different. Pick whichever you feel most comfortable with.

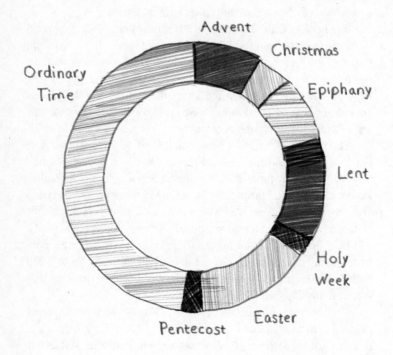

20

Embrace the calendar: it is color-coded!

Calendars seem to run our lives. We have to schedule our meetings, our dentist appointments, our children's soccer practices, and pray we do not forget our monthly supper club. So it may come as no surprise that the church also has its own calendar. And just like all the others, the church calendar marks seasons, special days, and the inevitable passage of time.

The church calendar seeks to use the passing of time as an avenue for reflecting on our relationship with God. The church year makes time holy and sacred. And it is not a linear construct, it is actually cyclical in nature. Each season marks an ending and a beginning. Each season brings to focus a different aspect of our spiritual life and relationship with God, and each transition is celebrated as a time of change and transformation.

As you ease into a worship tradition based on this calendar, there are helpful markers for remembering what season we are in: colors. The colors are symbolic of themes within the season, and they are used in and around the worship space to help us be mindful. For **Advent** (the beginning of the church year), we use blue. For **Christmas**, **Epiphany**, and **Easter**, we use white. For ordinary time, we use green. On particular celebration days, like the day of **Pentecost** or at the ordination of a deacon or priest, we use red.

21

Use the liturgy to cope with your complex past

Now, "liturgy" literally means the work of the people, so be advised—you are working. Church is not a concert or a show. When you participate in the liturgy of The Episcopal Church, there are things you have to do. This is why we have a Book of Common Prayer; it offers us a script to follow. Worshipping on Sunday requires being present and participatory. The good news is that it can be transformative. The liturgy offers a chance each Sunday to work through our past in the midst of our present. When we are young, life seems simple. We think our biggest danger is the monster under the bed. As we get older, the monster under the bed becomes manifest in broken relationships, complicated life events, loss, and behaviors and moments we often regret. We discover that life is actually quite complex, and our idyllic thoughts of the future do not match up with what we are experiencing. The past is often so weighty and rooted that it reaches right into our present life and overwhelms it.

Christians believe that God has dealt decisively with the past. God has absorbed the complexities of our pasts in Jesus. We are free to offer up the past to God and learn to live more fully in the present. This does not alleviate the consequences of the past, but it does alleviate the power of the past. And this is hard work, this is the work of the people, this is liturgy. Using the liturgy, especially the confession and the peace, to cope with the past is challenging. It will take more than one Sunday. But the gift of God is that we get to try it all over again each week, regardless of how well or poorly we did the week before.

22

Feel free to zone out from time to time

Yes, you read that correctly. It is alright to zone out from time to time. Sometimes we need the liturgy to just carry us. Sometimes watching the dancing flame of the candle or admiring the flowers or studying the stained glass in the window is the spiritual food that you need that morning. So let others say the prayers, provide the responses, and sing the hymns for us. This journey is hard work, it requires much of us, in fact all of us. It's exhausting! Our minds drift, our attention goes elsewhere, and before we know it we are in line for Eucharist and we have no idea how we got there.

Trust that God is big enough to hold it all, even the space cadet journey. God is capable of meeting us where we are, even when our body is in one physical space and our mind or heart is wandering elsewhere. Just be mindful you do not tell the preacher you didn't hear a word she said; that's a bit of bad form.

23

Sort through your selfishness, offer your selflessness

There are two parts to a typical service—the liturgy of the Word and the liturgy of Holy Communion. We listen to readings from the Bible, hear the sermon, and confess our brokenness to God during the Word. Then in Holy Communion, we journey through the suffering and sacrifice of Jesus, followed by the sharing of his body and blood. But before we can do that, we must do two things: we must sort out our selfishness and all those things that keep us from peace and love with ourselves and with each other, and we must be prepared to offer ourselves, even in our brokenness, to the work of God in Jesus.

Jesus tells us that before coming into the Father's presence, we must be sure that we are at peace with our neighbor (Matt. 5:23–24).

So, when we arrive at the Peace at the end of the liturgy of the Word, we must recognize the essential nature of what we are doing. In the immediate sense, we are reaching across the aisle to someone different from ourselves and offering them peace—that means reaching across and above cultural, economical, political, and social diversity in order to proclaim peace beyond difference. Often you will hear, "Peace be with you,"or, "God's peace," as this encounter spreads across the room. In the more big-picture sense, we are reaching into our past and making peace with all those people and moments that have caused us pain—that means letting go of resentment, ill will, bitterness, and hurt at the hands of another. We must take a hard look at what we think makes us different from others (selfishness at its core) and realize that in the end we are losing sight of the love project if we do not sort through it all and arrive at an attempt for peace.

The second thing we must do is offer our selflessness. The transition into the portion of the service for Holy Communion starts with the offering. This is the moment when we are invited to reflect on our attachment to "things". In the Gospel of Luke, Jesus exhorts us to give up our obsession with possessions. It is incredible how much our lives are dictated by the acquiring of things: money, objects, status, anything that differentiates us from another. During the offertory, we are invited to readjust our vision, to take stock of our lives, and to be reminded that all we have, all we are, all we ever will be are gifts from God. And in thanksgiving of that remembrance, we offer ourselves up to God and God's vision for our lives. We offer the bread and the wine from the community to the service, we offer a portion of our finances to support the work of the church, and we offer ourselves, renewed in efforts of peace and harmony, to participation in the work of the Gospel.

Mortgage

Career

Loneliness

Fear

24

Lift up your heart

The Eucharist, which means "thanksgiving," comes after the offertory. Again, we find ourselves participating in a communal act of praise through voice and body. This rule is taken from part of the opening dialogue. The **priest** invites the congregation to lift up their hearts, and the congregation responds by saying, "It is right to give God thanks and praise." We lift up our hearts in order to bring our spirits closer to the Divine. In all ways we are called to continually seek a deeper connection with God, but at this part of the liturgy on Sundays we are earnestly positioned toward it.

This is our weekly re-orientation toward all we should be thankful for. So often we take for granted the wonderful things in our lives—our families, our friends, our health. Unfortunately, until the status quo is challenged, we often go around feeling unfulfilled and dissatisfied in the world because we consider the miracle of breath and life and love as a given. In the Sunday liturgy, we are faced with the reality of our mistakes and fragility. In light of that, we are invited again to be thankful to God for all the wonderful, incredible things we have here and now. For that, it is right to give God thanks and praise.

25

It is right to give God thanks and praise . . . even in the tragic

Life sucks a lot of time. Illness and death are part of living. They just are. No one can dodge it. We will all at some time be sick; we will all have people in our lives who are sick; it is just the way it is.

Now this is the weird thing. At the heart of the Episcopal liturgy of Holy Communion is the Prayer of Great Thanksgiving. The celebrant takes us through a journey—we thank God for creation; we thank God for revealing to humanity the love project; and we thank God for not giving up on us even when we mess it up. Then it gets serious.

We are invited to give thanks for the death of Jesus—a young man who died a cruel and unjust death at the hands of the Roman authorities. We do so because in that act of dying on a cross, we believe that humanity was redeemed. We do so because we believe that God is in the tragic. We do so because Good Friday (when Jesus died on the cross) is always followed by Easter Sunday (when Jesus was resurrected and triumphs over death).

When life sucks we can respond to the challenge in one of two ways. We can get bitter and angry; or we can search for the signs of grace and hope. When we opt for the former, we make our challenges harder—our reaction exacerbates the pain. So instead, every week we practice hard to learn how to do the latter and we slowly learn how to cope constructively with the pain.

26

Believe that prayer works

Prayer is really important (see Rules 6, 29, 30, and 42). We should know that we are invited to pray in all times, in all places, with all effort (Philippians 4:6, Colossians 4:2, 1 Thessalonians 5:17). It is part of our relationship with God, when we attend to the connection with our creator and keep focused on what matters. Prayer is also our opportunity to bring our worries, concerns, and needs to God.

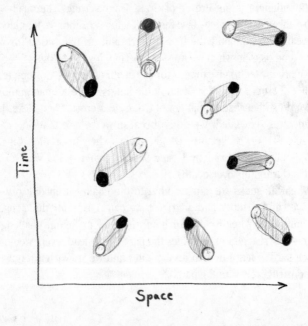

Yet, it might seem puzzling. Why does an all-powerful, all-knowing God need us to pray for anything? What can we tell God that God does not already know and can take into account when God decides to act? The answer is this: out of all the possible worlds that God could have created, God created this one. God created out of love a world designed for the flourishing of love. An act of love requires genuine freedom, and therefore a people who are genuinely free. So, in order to live into the love project, God requires our free cooperation in terms of both action and prayer. Our choice to pray for the triumph of love is just as integral in bringing about God's vision for this world as our actions are.

How we pray and who we pray with are equally important. It is good and right to pray for our own lives, personally and intimately. But part of the work of prayer also places our lives within the broader context of our community. Here, praying with a church community helps us locate our own worries within the envelope of the entire world's worries. We recognize that our stress over the hole we ripped in our pants is small in comparison to those without food, water, or shelter. Our outrage at someone honking their car horn at us is probably minimal in comparison with those who live in war-torn cities and villages. These are precious moments. These are moments when communal prayer brings us beyond ourselves into the workings of our world. And in this way, we are also living into Rule 14, because public, community prayer has been practiced in the Christian tradition since the second century.

One way to make sense of prayer is to think of it as a mechanism that creates space for God to do things. One great thing about quantum physics is that it allows us to understand the universe as an open, dynamic, and interconnected system. This reality and what we know of prayer work together to help us understand that there is space and need for divine action and human participation. When we pray—whether for healing, courage, strength, or peace—our insistence for love to overcome suffering creates avenues for divine action.

27

Don't just stand there, do something!

Each Sunday, you'll experience the ritual of the beloved announcements portion of the service. Person after person after person will get up in front of the congregation and ask for help and volunteers for all sorts of things. The food drive needs more canned goods. The habitat build needs more people to participate. The bake sale doesn't have enough cookies. Unfortunately, the reality is that very few people will actually pay attention and offer to help. So for heaven's sake, purely out of compassion if nothing else, don't just stand there! Do something! It will be more rewarding than you can imagine.

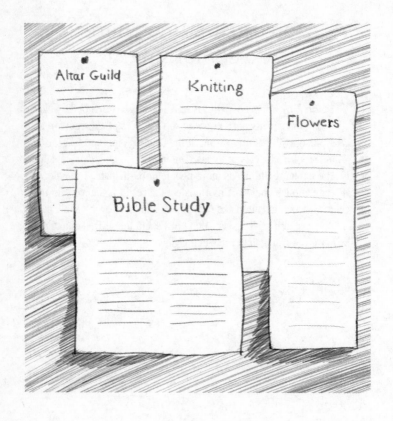

28

Play committee speed-dating

As you start to become a member of a worshipping community rather than an observer, the expansive avenues for involvement can become overwhelming. You want to get involved, but you don't know where to start. And, even if you aren't really sure if you want to get involved, chances are you will get asked to serve in one capacity or another. So, look around. The Episcopal Church loves committees and clubs. There are countless to choose from: book clubs, knitting clubs, altar guild, flower guild, Sunday school helpers, young adult groups, Bible studies, parish retreat committees, grounds committees, ushers, homeless outreach, and the list goes on. There is something for everyone; you just have to give a few a try!

Section Four

RULES FOR EVERY DAY

Faith does not start and end on Sundays. It goes into the week and transforms the week. This is **discipleship**—the act of following Jesus and seeking to live a life transformed by Jesus. Now the goal of discipleship is to live aware of the reality of God all around us. When we do this, we are more deliberate and more determined to transcend our propensities to egotism, selfishness, and preoccupation with the trivial. And instead we focus on the love project; we become agents of joy and hope.

Here are eleven rules that help orientate our lives toward God on a daily basis.

29

Start every day giving thanks for everything that is good

hank you! Thank you for reading this book. Thank you for giving us a chance to walk with you on this journey. Thank you for being willing to take a risk that offers eternal life in Jesus. Now . . . it's your turn. Go ahead, try it. Say thank you for something to someone.

How we approach a day is crucial. If we wake up angry, dissatisfied, frustrated, sick to death of our spouse, job, and life, then we will have a miserable day. If we start our day with gratitude for all the obvious things (we can see, smile, laugh, have a roof over our head, and have friends), then we are much more likely to have a good day. So the first rule of discipleship is to offer our thanks to God.

This act of giving praise and bringing awareness of everything that is good sets a tonal anchor for us as we continue throughout the rest of our day. It focuses our hearts and minds in a positive direction toward our God and our lives. Just as a Sunday worship service readjusts our vision toward who we are and whose we are, so starting each new day giving thanks reminds us, too. You'll be amazed at how different your day is when you start it with a measure of thankfulness.

30

Find space to be alone with God

This rule is a natural extension of the one that comes before it. Your relationship with God is in many ways just like any other relationship you have. It takes time, intention, and cultivation. Offering thanks for the blessings in your life is one of the ways

to acknowledge and appreciate the life-giving relationship you have with God. Now, the extension of that is to find time and space to enjoy God's company and companionship. Invest in your relationship by setting aside a piece of each day to be alone with God—dare to go on some dates! Take God out for a nice long walk along the beach, for a drive through the mountains, or on a bike ride down the street. Things do seem to be getting serious, after all!

Buy a copy of the Book of Common Prayer. You will then discover that the book isn't just for Sundays. There is a section called "Daily Devotions for Individuals and Families." There is a fifteen-minute or so abridged Morning Prayer that you could use. It is great for those times when you are in a rush. Another helpful resource is the *Daily Prayer for All Seasons*[2]—it is a journey through the church calendar with a short, manageable liturgy for eight moments in the day (individuals are encouraged to do at least one of those moments: groups might prefer the full monastic regime).

This time can look like many things—prayer, exploring Scripture, enjoying nature, or a host of other things. Think about your journey to faith and what brought you to that place of transcendence and spiritual awakening. Those parts of your journey can be helpful here in finding ways to spend time with God. The trick is to do it each day. There's no such thing as a spiritual piggy bank or roll-over minutes, so you can't collect bonus points to save up for a day off. This is the nitty-gritty, in-and-out, daily battle for your heart and soul.

---

2. Standing Commission on Liturgy and Music, *Daily Prayer for All Seasons* (New York: Church Publishing, 2014).

31

Let God in

Most of us are pretty complicated. We are bundles of fear, insecurity, and damaged egos. We try to sort ourselves out. We read self-help books, go to the gym, and have a therapist. And those resources can be helpful and useful. The truth is, however, that we can still find ourselves hurting others and not coping well when life gets hard.

So this rule is simple: God wants to help. But we need to give God space to help. God needs time with us. God needs to allow the triggers to be exposed so they can be healed. One popular biblical metaphor is the potter and the clay (see Jeremiah 18, Isaiah 64:8, and Romans 9:21). God is the potter and we are the clay. And God wants to take our lives and make something beautiful out of them. Our goal is to give God the space to do that.

32

Watch for "ice on bridge"

Life is hard. People make mistakes, do terrible things, and are indifferent to others. We like to imagine that Christians are different, but the truth is Christians are as messed up as everyone else. The only difference is that we are trying hard to let God help us.

In this rule, we want to emphasize the need to watch for damaging triggers that hurt those close to us. It is so weird, really, how we tend to make difficult situations even more difficult for ourselves. We are in an argument with a friend and know bringing up a certain topic will be hurtful to them, but we do so anyway. Or we know that staying late at the office every day is damaging to our marriage and our relationship with our children, but our addiction to work drives us to stay late anyway and lets our relationships suffer for doing so. Or we spread gossip and call it "concern for others." In all these ways, and in many more, we are hurting those close to us.

So—look ahead. Read the warning signs. Think through outcomes and consequences. We are created to love and be loved. When we hurt those around us, we are not living into the fullness of our created intention. We are living into sinful tendencies—to use good, old fashioned language. So, beware of "ice on bridge"—do everything you can to live into the Gospel and be especially mindful of the ripple effect each of your actions causes in the world around you. Think especially of the people who surround you.

33

Beware the apple

So think here of Snow White or Adam and Eve, when reading this rule. A key part of the love project is to avoid situations that can mess us up. This is the realm of temptation (to use traditional language again), the doorway into sin.

OK, this is really just common sense. But let us state it. The best way to steer clear of damaging ourselves and those we love is to avoid certain situations—in other words, beware the apple. This is the phrase to remember: "This might be a bad idea." If you say that to yourself, chances are that it probably *is* a bad idea! You think your married coworker is attractive? Don't schedule overnight business trips with just the two of you. You know you enjoy ice cream more than salad? Don't keep ice cream in the house. You have an intense desire to make sure your neighbor's cat will never use your yard as a litter box again? Walk away from the BB gun. The best way to attend to our interior lives and cultivate healthy, loving lives is to walk away from temptation.

34

Spiritual direction is cool and strictly confidential

Spiritual direction is one of the most underused resources in our spiritual development and formation. How interesting that more and more leaders of the church are calling for more of it! It is a wonderful opportunity to allow a trained, caring, faithful individual to help you seek out and identify God's presence in your life. This is a place to spend time reflecting on your spiritual encounters and issues. Reflection is a key part of the formation and growth process. In Spiritual Direction, we are able to work through our daily faith experiences with a guide who is there to help. And if we're being candid . . . how cool is it to sit and ponder the divine interactions in your life? It is spiritually stimulating, intellectually stimulating, emotionally stimulating.

And—it is confidential. All those apples and warning signs you struggle with on a spiritual level are fair game to sort through in spiritual direction. Does God really care if you lust after a fictional character? Is God watching you when you sin? How do you figure out if bad things happen to good people for a reason? Did God help me get that job or was it luck, skill, my own resolve, etc? Spiritual Direction is a wonderful place to explore the complexity and depth of the intersection of life and faith. Give it a try. Give it two tries, in fact. It is cool, we promise. And even if it is not, at least it is confidential.

35

Return your shopping cart at the grocery store

Alright—now we come to the tough stuff. Keep your middle finger down. What your mother said is still true, "If you can't say anything nice, don't say anything at all." Stand up on the bus so an elderly or differently-abled person may have a seat. Always say please and thank you. And for goodness sake, return your shopping cart! No one likes to pull into a parking space only to realize it's already occupied by the remnants of a previous store patron. Ugh.

Discipleship is about the little, everyday things. Change doesn't happen in grand gestures, it happens in the immeasurable moments we experience day in and day out. This is where the rubber meets the road in our faith journey. Do we believe what we say on Sundays? Do we act out the love and faith we read about in the Bible and believe to be true? Are we really loving our neighbors as ourselves? Even if our neighbor is the car that just cut us off on the interstate? These repetitive acts are the moments that birth habits—we get to choose whether they are birthed in short-sighted anger, frustration, and hurt, or in compassion, patience, and love. And when you struggle with which direction to go, give a nod to Rule 7: remember it's all about the love project.

36

Learn to give—intentionally and seriously

This is part of the language of stewardship—acting responsibly with the assets and gifts we've been given. We need to be good stewards—and no, we don't mean like the Stewards of Gondor (please introduce yourself to J.R.R. Tolkien and have your literary world rocked if that reference means nothing to you).

There are many ways to be a good steward, and the next few rules explore some of the ways that we give of ourselves intentionally and seriously in order to be responsible patrons of our gifts and talents. We need to learn to give of ourselves to God and to others. We need to recognize that who we are and what we have are themselves gifts that we should share with others.

Giving helps us focus on what matters. When we decide we cannot afford to give or we would rather spend the extra on that gadget or outfit or trip, we are getting our priorities wrong. Relationships are what matter; things and stuff are trivial. The scratch on the new car and the food stain that won't come out of your favorite shirt are irrelevant. The moment scratches and stains matter then we know we have our priorities all wrong. If you don't have a new car and you don't buy such expensive clothes, then the scratches and stains won't matter. So do the right thing: find someone who (or some organization that) needs that money and give that money to them.

We are always short of money. When we are in college, we are trying to get by paycheck to paycheck (even though we always find money for the ice cream trip); when we are working, we have a car to run, children to educate, and a mortgage to pay (even though we always find the money for a vacation). So just make it a rule: give 10 percent—it is a good rule.

37

Commit to doing something for others

Jesus tells this remarkable parable about the sheep and the goats. Those who have everlasting life are those who see Jesus in the poor, homeless, naked, and in prison (Matt. 25:34–40). This parable is crystal clear (Rule 11 sure is coming in handy)—we must take care of each other. This is a particular shade of stewardship, one colored by acts of service and sacrifices of time and self. Commit, with time, energy, money, and resources, to doing something for someone else. Organize a food or clothing drive. Volunteer at a local soup kitchen. Read to kids for an hour every week at the public library in your neighborhood.

Often we like to confine our service to those who are most like us. Resist this temptation. Make sure your service to others takes you to places where you are surrounded by people who are different. Part of the way we do that is by serving those around us in a way that recognizes and honors their dignity and humanity. There is nothing that separates us save cultural and social constructs—and Jesus calls us into a way of life that does not let those constructs define us.

38

Recycle, don't add to landfills, turn off lights, and walk

This one is sort of self-explanatory, really. Just as we are called to be good stewards of our gifts, time, and talents, we are also called to a more communal stewardship, that of caring for God's creation. Our prayer book has a really lovely way of describing our planet: this fragile earth, our island home. And it is fragile. We must take care to treat it well. Save electricity. Recycle whatever and whenever you can. Plant some trees. We must all do our part to make sure the beautiful creation that surrounds us is sustained and cultivated for those who come after us.

39

Eat and drink wisely

Again, this is a form of creation stewardship. Just as we take care of others—people, animals, and the environment—so we must take care of ourselves. Loving our neighbors as ourselves doesn't work very well if we don't actually love ourselves. Therefore eat and drink wisely. Consume in moderation. The journalist Michael Pollan has it exactly right when he says, "If it came from a plant, eat it; if it was made in a plant, don't."[3] Be careful of excess indulgences. This is the only body you get; treat it well.

---

3. Michael Pollan, *Food Rules* (New York: Penguin Group, 2009), 41.

40

Say grace, give grace, receive grace

Grace is a Christian buzz word. But what does it mean? Grace is the recognition that in the end it is all God; God is the one that does all the work. And we kid ourselves when we imagine that we are making a significant contribution without God. So God is the one who created us, loved us, redeemed us, and is attempting to transform us into agents of hope and love. God is the one who is constantly working behind the scenes to bring possibilities to hopeless and tragic situations. And God does all this, not because we deserve it (because we don't—we spend most of our time putting up roadblocks to God), but out of grace.

Give grace—we need to be gentle with others. Everyone messes up. So learn to forgive (repeatedly), be understanding, and be kind. And receive grace—we need to be able to let others forgive us.

So pause before every meal and say "grace." Say thank you for the miracle of the meal before you. Unless you planted, grew, harvested, cleaned, and cooked everything on your table at a meal, you are enjoying your supper due to the work of others. And the labor of others was made possible by the God who provides the gift of being from every second to every second. Grace is at the heart of the divine love project. Get used to it.

Section Five

RULES FOR WHEN LIFE IS HARD

One of the most religious places in the world is a hospice. When you are actually suffering, prayer becomes the lifeline. When you are young, sitting perhaps in a philosophy seminar, the problem of evil and suffering is a clear refutation of the existence of God. Why does a good and all-powerful God allow evil and suffering? The question is so simple and so unanswerable. For the young and healthy, it is clear evidence that God does not exist.

The paradox of suffering is that it is in the midst of pain that one sees things most clearly. When you are young and healthy, you worry about all the things that do not matter—the zit, the need for the Apple Watch, recognition, and status. When you suffer, you suddenly see how stupid all those worries are. You are invited to focus on what really matters—the gift of life, the gift of a few more days, months, and years, the gift of relationships with those around you, and the extraordinary gift of days that are pain-free and just normal. As you strip away silly concerns, you encounter the nature of life at its most fundamental. And you feel God more intimately than at any other time.

The truth about suffering is that it is often the norm. Unhappy families are everywhere; insecure employees who are finding their work unfulfilling are the norm; and countless women and men are living with chronic pain and illness—both mental and physical.

Coping when life is hard is where faith comes in handy. Here are five rules that can help you cope.

41

It is OK to be mad at God

Psalm 137 is all about a people who have been uprooted from their homes, dragged into exile, and are bitter and angry at God. They all complain: "How can you sing the Lord's song in a strange land?" The extent and depth of their bitterness comes out right at the end, "O daughter Babylon, you devastator! Happy shall they be who pay you back what you have done to us! Happy shall they be who take your little ones and dash them against the rock!" Just feel the rage. Here is a plea for revenge where the psalmist hopes that the Babylonian babies are killed by dashing them against the rocks.

It is a shocking psalm. But it is a reassuring psalm. There are moments in our lives when we need to be angry. We need to be mad with God. We need to scream, shout, and complain. We need to release all the pain and let God know. And guess what? God can handle it. God is not offended.

The pain we are facing is real. It hurts. It makes living so hard and difficult. This rule invites us to recognize that reality. And if we need to use a few expletives, then that is OK as well.

Prayer

42

Keep the prayer simple—ask just for the strength to cope

Praying when you are hurting is hard. It is often really unclear exactly what you are praying for. The apostle Paul in Romans 8:26 explains that "the Spirit helps us in our weakness; for we do not know how to pray as we ought, but that very Spirit intercedes with sighs too deep for words." There are moments when we are at our weakest, when we need the Holy Spirit to do the praying for us. So as we sit in the presence of God, the fewer words the better. Just let the Holy Spirit pray for you.

Often when life is hard, the challenge is simply getting through the next day. So the axiom "one day at a time" is a good one. We need the strength to cope to get through the next twenty-four hours still sane and hopeful. Sanity and hopefulness are often two really important miracles that are desperately needed.

43

Let others be there for you as you will be there for others

Watching a loved one suffer is hard. We want to help. It is sometimes hard to see what we can do, but something, anything, is the need.

As we walk through our hard, difficult season of pain, it is important to recognize that this empathy and love are gifts that should be graciously received. Receive the card, note, and e-mail. Receive with gratitude the prayers. Accept the offer of those who would like to cook for you. Let the guest visit for a while. Jesus said, "In everything do to others as you would have them do to you" (Matt. 7:12). There is a cosmic golden rule in operation here. The young and healthy are granted the opportunity to serve and support those who are older and dying; and one day, the young will be dying and will need the next generation to be there for them. Graciousness is the key. We need to be gracious in the offer of help; and we need to be gracious in the receiving of those offers of help.

44

Remember God has been where you are

Remember Rule 25. When we live in the world of the Bible, we learn that suffering is everywhere. The psalms are full of pain; the people of God are often finding life hard. From the personal to the institutional, suffering is everywhere. Going to church forces you to think about suffering a great deal.

Although suffering is a major biblical theme, the reason for suffering is never fully explained. We don't know why God allows suffering and evil in the creation. But the Christian claim is this: even though we don't have an explanation for suffering, we do know that God knows what suffering involves; God has felt the pain of loss. The extraordinary gift of Good Friday is that we learn that God Almighty took human form and died at the hands of the creation that God made. And this death was cruel, harsh, and painful. Christianity doesn't give you a head answer about suffering, but it does give you a heart answer. As we suffer, we are invited to meditate afresh on the suffering of Jesus—the very embodiment of God in our midst.

45

Trust that ultimately God promises it will be OK

Remember God works on a vast canvas. God created this universe (perhaps along with many other universes) 13.7 billion years ago. Our sun will not die for another 5 million years. God has the big picture. We, on the other hand, are very local and immediate. Our canvas is days, weeks, and months. We certainly do not see beyond a lifetime—or at least do not do so easily.

The good news is that there is nothing that can happen to us on earth that God will not ultimately make sure is OK. Often things get better after weeks, months, or years. And eventually we are a cancer survivor or a new relationship forms that is healing or we find more satisfying employment. But sometimes the OK moment comes with the release from this life and a passing into the loving cosmic embrace of God.

It is important to give God all the options. Sometimes we just have to trust that God knows best for us in hard situations.

Section Six

RULES FOR COOL EPISCOPALIANS

Christians often do not help themselves. To continue to question the theory of evolution over 150 years after the publication of *The Origin of the Species* is just untenable. To insist that everyone else, apart from your sect, is on the way to hell is very implausible. To treat beliefs like a big package that one cannot question or modify is ridiculous. And this is where Episcopalians are really cool. We get all this. So you are joining a club which will invite and welcome your questions, thoughts, doubts, and issues. In fact, wherever you are on the journey, The Episcopal Church welcomes you.

46

Ask questions; have doubts

Remember God is a complicated topic. Complicated topics lend themselves to debates, questions, and provisional positions. Naturally, some ideas are more sure than others. Our experience of the transcendent in our lives makes us aware of the reality of God, but we can legitimately debate the existence of demons.

Never be afraid of questions. Never be afraid of doubts. Never be afraid of the atheist critiques of Christianity. God can handle questions, doubts, and atheists. Episcopalians do not fear that they will suddenly lose their faith because an atheist will make a point that leaves them dumbfounded. In fact, it can be quite affirming to faith to have to sort through questions and arguments that we are initially unable to answer.

As one studies the history of Christianity, one finds a pattern. The tradition is a dialogue between the core conviction that God is revealed in Jesus and the ever-changing discoveries humans are learning about the world. Early Christianity was a combination of **Hellenistic** culture (think Greeks) and Hebrew culture; then in the fourth century, Augustine of Hippo shaped Christianity in conversation with the **neoplatonism** of his day; then in the thirteenth century, Thomas Aquinas learned of Aristotle from Muslims and formulated the faith afresh. Like science, mathematics, and economics, Christianity changes and develops. An important agent of such development is our questions and doubts.

47

You can be evangelical or liberal or Anglo-Catholic or low church or put your hands in the air or just want choral music all the time

Episcopal churches do have certain basics in common. The Book of Common Prayer is a script that we all follow. But built on that foundation is tons of variety. Some Episcopalians are evangelical (they stress the importance of individual salvation); others are Anglo-Catholic (they love elaborate liturgy and use incense); others again are low church (they think it important to keep liturgy very simple); and when it comes to music—some love the praise band and others enjoy the traditional choral tradition of Anglicanism.

In fact the choices can get even more interesting. There are congregations that specialize in social justice and make outreach ministries the priority; others love Christian formation and have a university of educational options in between the services; and others have a fabulous music program and a choir that is amazing.

We like the differences among congregations. After all, we are not all the same. It is good to find just the right niche for you.

48

Appreciate the beauty of the Lessons and Carols service

Now this won't be everyone's cup of tea, so this is an optional rule. But at least give it a go. It was a service invented by King's College at the University of Cambridge in 1918 and now it is found at practically every cathedral in the United States. Normally, it features Advent carols, but sometimes you can get the Christmastide version.

And it is quite moving. It is just readings from the Bible and carols—a sublime combination of Scripture and music. Normally, it is nine lessons telling the story of salvation history from the creation to incarnation, and after each lesson there is a beautiful carol.

It is an extraordinary service, beautiful in its simplicity. This is the Anglican choral tradition at its finest.

49

Your building tells a story— listen to it!

Increasingly you can find congregations of The Episcopal Church everywhere. Some meet in a warehouse; others in a coffee shop; and others again outside in a park. But most older congregations still meet in a traditional church building. And the building is part of the message.

Often the shape is cruciform (i.e. shaped like a cross). You sit in the middle of the sacred symbol of Christianity. Then the furniture is special. Often on arrival you walk past the font (our admission into the family of God through baptism). The pulpit is the place for the preaching of the Word. The altar is normally given some prominence because this is where we celebrate the Eucharist. Then we have stained glass. The windows are worth studying. And in every congregation there is someone who has made the windows a focus of their ministry. The themes embedded in the windows can be remarkably varied. Sometimes the focus is scenes from the life of Jesus; at other times, parables are prominent; and sometimes, there is a distinctive local or regional emphasis that is the priority.

People get very attached to their buildings. The space in which women and men struggle with their prayers—hopes and fears—and renew their commitment to the love project is special. The energy of the people of God leaves a mark on the space, which can be felt by those who come and visit.

50

You don't have to believe every-one else is going to hell

OK. Theology 101. We learn about God from Jesus of Nazareth. And as we look at the words and deeds of Jesus, we learn of a God of love that meets us wherever we are. It is true that Jesus talked about hell. For Jesus, it is the rich and powerful that are in trouble in the afterlife. When Jesus tells the parable about the rich man and Lazarus, it is the rich man who ends up in torment (Luke 16:19–31). For Jesus, it isn't sex or heresy that gets us to hell, but how we treat each other.

Some Christians like to insist that the only folks in heaven are those who are "observant Roman Catholics" or have been "born again." Some Christians talk as if only their sect will make it; the rest of us are burning in the fiery flames of hell. Yet this is not what we learn from Jesus.

Episcopalians tend to a theology of generosity. We learn from Jesus that God is more interested in transforming our lives than condemning. And given that most of us reflect the religion of the culture into which we were born, God would never condemn to hell a human life who just happened to be born into a predominantly non-Christian culture. So you can save all that hellfire and brimstone for your next game of Scrabble if you wish.

51

Honor God in all things, even sex

Christians get bad press because we are constantly going on about sex. And The Episcopal Church has led the way with its focus on sex over the last decade. However, a rule is now emerging which is a clear and healthy step forward.

Our official line is now this: we understand that folks have different orientations. So now we are more focused on the quality of the relationship. We believe in faithful, monogamous relationships, where the focus is the joy of giving of ourselves to each other in an intimate way. The Episcopal Church does permit same sex marriages and blessings.

The Episcopal Church continues to recognize that many members still disagree with the official line. This is good. If theology is complicated, then so is ethics. And we need the range of voices as we seek to discern the way forward for our church.

52

Relax about science—
evolution is OK

Science is cool. You will not find Episcopalians believing that there is a massive conspiracy among biologists working in the finest universities of the United States, who know the creationists are right but the scientific establishment has too much invested in the "lie" of evolution. Genesis tells us why the world was created; evolution tells us how. It is as simple as that.

Science is actually really exciting. One puzzle for contemporary cosmologists is why the universe looks "fixed." It looks like the universe always knew that life was coming. Just to take one illustration: for life to emerge the gravitational pull and the acceleration at the big bang had to be in perfect balance; in fact, so perfect it is the equivalent of a person taking a gun and hitting a target on the other side of the observable universe. So really, really balanced! And this is just one of almost thirty factors that had to be just right. The "**anthropic principle**," as it is called, has provoked considerable discussion. Naturally persons of faith are not surprised by this discovery. We always knew that God intended life to emerge. Indeed, the more you know about science and religion, the clearer it is that they are not actually at odds with one another. So it is OK to value them both.

53

You can think some things in the Bible probably didn't happen

Did Adam and Eve really exist as historic human beings? Did God really flood the entire world at the time of Noah? Did the walls of Jericho really come tumbling down because folks marched around them seven times? Will Jesus meet the redeemed in the sky at the second coming? And the answer is: probably not. And that is just fine. Our faith tradition is such that contradictions, the certainty of particular events, and archaeological evidence (or the lack thereof) do not render the Bible incomprehensible. Treat it under the umbrella of Rule 46; it is OK to have questions and doubts. It is harder to struggle through these things than to accept them at face value. But it is often more rewarding. So if you do not think the valley of the dry bones actually happened, that is alright (Ezek. 37:1–14). Don't worry about it.

54

Learn about the Eucharist— it really is the presence of Christ Jesus

Pretty rapidly you will learn that for most Episcopalians you haven't really been to church unless you have taken the Eucharist. Simply gathering to praise and pray to God are not enough. Instead, we try every week to receive the Holy Mysteries—a tool for transformed living that we are invited to receive into our lives.

Why is the Eucharist so important? It is important on many levels. First, it is table fellowship (the family are gathering around the table to share a meal). It represents our unity in Christ. Second, Episcopalians believe that in a real sense Christ is present in the bread and wine. The Eternal Word that entered Jesus of Nazareth becomes manifest in the bread and wine to make Christ present to us. Therefore when we receive the sacrament it really is divine life that can help us with the love project.

55

Somewhere there is an Anglican theologian who agrees with you—so relax

Week in, week out we follow the book. We follow the script in the book. The responses become part of us. And perhaps because of this grounding, the Anglican tradition (of which The Episcopal Church is a part) has birthed a lively intellectual tradition that goes in every conceivable direction.

If you are very conservative, read James Packer—he believes that the Bible is without error; if you are very liberal, read John Shelby Spong—he does not believe in the Incarnation nor the Trinity and is skeptical about theism. If you have strong sympathies with feminism, then Kathryn Tanner is really good. If you like **postmodernism**, then you will like John Milbank. If you are interested in reconciliation and forgiveness, then you will love Miroslav Volf.

How can one tradition embrace such diversity? Remember the assumptions we make about God: God is complicated. It is inevitable that there will be a lively debate about the nature of God because the subject matter is complicated. And The Episcopal Church shares a liturgy that helps us live with amazing intellectual diversity.

56

Feel the connection with the ninety million Anglicans around the globe

When you become an Episcopalian, you automatically join a much larger club—the Anglican Communion. In fact, it is the third largest club in christendom. (The largest club is the Roman Catholic church; and in second place are the Orthodox churches.) It means that men and women in over 165 countries are part of our tradition. We recognize as our spiritual head the Archbishop of Canterbury in England.

We are primarily an African church. Numerically our strength is in the global south. But we also have a significant presence in Asia, Australia, and of course Europe.

This means that there are lots of opportunities for travel; most dioceses and many congregations have partners in other countries around the communion. It also means that you find many guests from the communion coming to the United States. It makes us a global family with a sensitivity for the hopes and challenges facing our sisters and brothers overseas.

57

Learn to laugh at yourself— Episcopalians are good at that

Q: How many Episcopalians does it take to change a light bulb?
A: Ten. One to actually change the bulb and nine to say how much they like the old one.

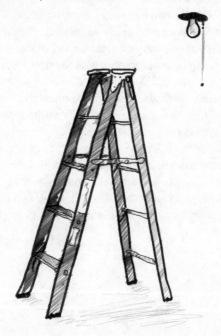

Q: How many Episcopalians does it take to change a light bulb?

A: Twelve. One to do the work and eleven to serve on a committee.

Q: How many Episcopalians does it take to change a light bulb?

A: Change that light bulb? My grandmother donated that light bulb.

Or here is one which is more complicated (and very inside the tribe):

So a massive meteorite is about to hit the planet and destroy everyone on earth. There is nothing like the end of the world to bring folks out to church. So a Baptist minister, a Roman Catholic priest, and an Episcopal priest meet up and are trying to decide what text they should preach on at the services that every church is holding that night. The Baptist goes first: He says, "It has to be John 3 verse 16: 'For God so loved the world that he gave his only Son.'" He goes on: "I am going to bring people to Jesus tonight." The Roman Catholic priest goes second. He says, "I am going to preach on Matthew 16 verse 18, where Jesus explains to Peter that he is the first Pope and that there is one true Church in Christendom and that is the Roman Catholic Church and that everyone in the congregation needs to be in good standing in Mother Church." Then they both look at the Episcopal priest. "What are you going to preach on?" they asked. The Episcopal priest replies, "I will preach on the lectionary readings for the day."

And finally,

Q: Why do Episcopalians always sit on the back row at church?

A: Because there are no seats in the parking lot.

You get the idea.

God is on the
side of the poor

58

Recognize that we must do everything we can for the poor and the marginalized

Surprise. **Jesus rarely talks about sex,** but talks endlessly about the poor and the marginalized. We tend to focus on the sex because it is easier than all this talk of "selling everything you have and giving it to the poor." But given our theology, we have no way we can avoid this one. If Jesus discloses to us God—in words and deeds, then Jesus' preoccupation with the poor makes the poor God's priority. So there you have it. We have no choice but to make God's priority our priority.

Take an interest in politics, get involved in outreach ministries, and do everything you can for the poor and marginalized in society. This is God's rule.

59

Listen to the poets

Episcopalians love their poetry. Whether it is W. H. Auden or T. S. Eliot, the poet finds it easier to talk about the mystery of God than a philosopher. Episcopalians tend to be very modest when speaking about their faith. It is difficult to reduce the mystery of God down to a tag line on a button. So let us just listen carefully to the poets.

GRACE

The woods is shining this morning.
Red, gold and green, the leaves
lie on the ground, or fall,
or hang full of light in the air still.
Perfect in its rise and in its fall, it takes
the place it has been coming to forever.
It has not hastened here, or lagged.
See how surely it has sought itself,
its roots passing lordly through the earth.
See how without confusion it is
all that it is, and how flawless
its grace is. Running or walking, the way
is the same. Be still. Be still.
"He moves your bones, and the way is clear."[4]

—Wendell Berry

Along with the poets, we love our artists—from Leonardo da Vinci's famous *Last Supper* to Michelangelo's *The Creation of Adam* to John August Swanson's *Daniel.* We have already noted how valuable musicians are in opening up the transcendent. So along with the poets, enjoy all the arts.

---

4. Wendell Berry, "Grace," *http://www.poetryfoundation.org/poetrymagazine/browse/110/3#!/20598141.* June 1967.

Section Seven

RULES FOR HANGING AROUND EPISCOPALIANS

So you are beginning to get acquainted with The Episcopal Church, you are learning all the cool things about being an Episcopalian, and you are doing your best to get involved in the life of your church community. This means you are going to be spending more time with your Episcopal brothers and sisters. You are entering into the life of the "tribe." Just as with any unique culture, this church body has its own quirks and characteristics; we have our own language, dress code, attendance patterns, and ecosystem of connections and networks. Without some sense of what you are walking into, this can be a very overwhelming reality. Allow us to help you obtain some foundational knowledge for use in this new community.

Here are five rules to help you adjust to the Episcopal tribe life and relate to all those other people you encounter on Sunday mornings and throughout the week.

60

Learn the basic vocabulary

If you decide to study chemistry, you have to learn a new vocabulary (words like "distillation" and "diatomic"); if you decide to appreciate opera, you have to learn about "aria" and "bel canto." And getting into The Episcopal Church requires the same process.

It is part of joining a new tribe. Here are some basic terms. The Episcopal Church is organized geographically into units called **dioceses**. Each church within a particular region belongs to the same diocese, and each diocese is run by a bishop. A **verger** is usually a person who is not ordained who helps in the ordering of church services. They help form the procession, guide readers to the lectern, and generally keep things running smoothly. **Liturgy**, as we briefly touched on earlier, literally means the work of the people. It is the form by which we order our worship. A **canticle** is a hymn or psalm or other song of praise typically used in our church services and is made up of biblical text. A **vestry** is the governance of an individual church. It is made up of people from the church who meet regularly to discuss structural concerns like finances, building maintenance, and parish programming and effectiveness. A **chasuble** is the outermost piece of clothing a priest wears when celebrating the Eucharist. It sort of looks like a big drape and is color-coded according to the season (see Rule 20).

This list should help you get started in translating the Episco-ese of the tribe. Just like any other language, the only way to learn it is to practice. If you feel so inclined, here are some words for homework: lector, genuflect, narthex, undercroft, acolyte, and thurible.

And if all else fails, it is alright to ask someone to explain what they are talking about; fluency is never a prerequisite for membership.

61

Give everyone in your congregation a chance

We are an increasingly diverse denomination: there are historically African American congregations; there are growing numbers of Latino/a congregations; and there are congregations of every size and shape.

It is also true that The Episcopal Church is one of the oldest denominations in the United States. We have an impressive history. George Washington was an Episcopalian. Families that have ancestors on the *Mayflower* are part of The Episcopal Church. We have had more senators and congressmen than any other denomination.

So this is the rule: give everyone in your congregation a chance. Search for people who are different from you. Get to know your fellow churchgoers; listen for their interests and their passions, their pursuits and goals. Like all networks, the congregational network can help with both employment and hobbies. It is likely that someone around you loves reading biographies as much as you do or needs an extra player on their recreational kickball team. These are all ways to make connections and develop more robust networks within your church.

62

Enjoy dressing down on a Sunday, even though everyone else dresses up

We like our "Sunday best" attire in The Episcopal Church. Each Sunday, you'll find most churchgoers with pressed pants, pearls around their necks, or their Sunday brunch shoes. The Easter uniform includes seersucker and bowties in many places for the gentlemen, and beautifully colored dresses and hats for the ladies.

But don't let that stop you. Dress down every once in a while (or all the time)! Not only is it vastly more comfortable than those suspenders or that pencil skirt you were thinking about wearing, it is also a good reminder that The Episcopal Church welcomes you, just as you are, and that God meets you in the midst of whatever you are going through, regardless of possessions or outward appearance. So lose the tie, forget about those high heels, put on some jeans and sandals, and revel in how freeing it can be to worship in your comfy clothes!

63

Don't let yourself make the mistake of thinking we are a winter religion even if thousands of Episcopalians do take the summer off

It is the church's worst kept secret—attendance at Episcopal parishes is highest in the winter and lowest in the summer. But don't be fooled—we might have a church calendar that operates on a slightly different set of seasons than the traditional calendar, but that does not mean we take the summer off!

The unfortunate truth is that during the summer people go on vacation, kids are out of school, and Sundays are suddenly reserved for sleeping in or visiting the farmers' market. But be assured, we do indeed worship all year round. The thing to be cautious of in the summer is that because attendance wanes, the service schedule often changes. Instead of services at 7:45, 9:15 and 11:00 am, a church might instead offer services at 8:00 and 10:00 am during the summer. We recognize that this is confusing and not very welcoming, but you have a head start by knowing about it now. And, that 10:00 am service means you will get to know other people who go to a different service and will hopefully have a shorter wait at that new brunch place down the street!

64

Be gentle with the grumpy people in the parish because one day you will be the grumpy one (always use the Golden Rule)

This is true of just about every church in America, but it is worth stating: most Episcopal churches are multigenerational. They are made up of children, twentysomethings and thirtysomethings, seasoned professionals, and an increasing number of retired and older adults. Here's the thing: when you've been part of a church for your whole life—regardless of how long that life has been—you get very comfortable. Comfortableness often means we let down our guards and let some of our inner selves shine through, even when those inner selves are not very saintly. We get grumpy and irritable, we hate change that threatens our understanding of the way things are done, and sometimes we complain incessantly. The longer someone has been part of the church, it seems, the more likely this is to be true.

The Golden Rule is of great value in these moments, because the likelihood is that one day you will be the grumpy person in the church, and it will be hurtful and upsetting to go unheard, unacknowledged, and unaffirmed in your concerns for the church (even if they do come across as just being grumpy or irritable).

So, be patient. Be kind. Listen. There is much wisdom in the hearts of our longest attending members, and there are rich opportunities to learn from and be challenged by them. And one day, it will be you on the other end of the conversation, and someone else will have the option to be kind and patient and thoughtful, too.

Section Eight

RULES FOR REMEMBERING THE BIG PICTURE

Finally, we are in the home stretch. We remind ourselves of the basic rules for living a faithful life. Discipleship has its hard and bruising moments. And in this section, we remind ourselves of the fundamentals—stay in touch with God, stay in touch with the transforming power of forgiveness, and stay in touch with the congregations that make up The Episcopal Church.

65

Learn to forgive both yourself and others

Forgiveness is definitely a divine idea. There is no way a regular human could have come up with the idea. Forgiveness is the secret weapon of the Christian.

The act of forgiving another is powerful. When someone has wronged you, the temptation (literally) is to bear the grudge, to hate, to simmer in rage, and to plot revenge. And suddenly the wrong is amplified a million times. Our reaction to the wrong means the wrong continues to cast a long shadow over everything we do. But forgiveness is a radical act. It frees you up from the shadow. It keeps the wrong contained. It moves your head from a preoccupation with the past to create possibilities for the future.

And forgiveness is not confined simply to others. The same principle applies to ourselves. We will mess up. And we have a choice: we can forever beat ourselves up or we can trust that we are forgiven by the God who loves us. And once we learn to forgive both ourselves and others, we are freed up to live fully in the present and create a new future.

We believe in one Lord, Jesus Christ, the only
...olly begotten of the Father, God from G...
from Light true God from true God begotten, not m...
of one Being with the Father. Through him all things
made. For us and for our salvation he came down fr...
heaven by the power of the Holy Spirit he became in...
nate from the Virgin Mary, and was made man. For our
was crucified under Pontius Pilate; he suffered death...
was buried. On the third day he rose again in accorda...

66

Enjoy the fact that there is a familiar service in most towns in America

Eighty percent of services in Episcopal churches around the country are basically the same every single week. They are all out of the Book of Common Prayer, either Rite 1 or Rite 2. The sermon and music will obviously vary, but apart from that there will be a delightful familiarity. Even if the sermon is a problem, then the rest of the service is just out of the book. And when traveling—whether for vacations or business—you can enjoy a service most of which you will recognize.

Over time, the benefits of this will become apparent. The liturgy gets inside of you. It becomes part of the furniture of your mind. We learn to say from memory parts of the liturgy—the creed, the prayer of confession, and the post-communion prayer. We can dip into these parts of the liturgy whenever we need to do so.

Being a Christian is the act of seeing the world as intended by an agent of love; being an Episcopalian is learning to live with a liturgy that can connect you with the Love that sustains us at every single moment.

67

Remember it is all about God

Once you are in the middle of this journey of faith it is very easy to lose sight of the big picture. There will be moments when all you can see are the challenges in your life or the chaos in your church or the immediate muddle right in front of you.

Perspective—this is the key. Remember we believe in a God who shaped a universe that is 13.7 billion years old. Remember that living on planet earth right now are 7.3 billion people. Remember it is likely that there are sentient creatures on other planets. Perhaps there are other universes and the number of lives being sustained by God is phenomenal. And remember at the core of all creation, whether it is one universe or a hundred universes, is the Love Project.

Perspective helps. It locates our immediate worries. It also helps us to learn that most basic faith skill—the skill of trust. God has been around an awfully long time; God will take us through this season surrounding us with love and peace. Just trust.

Glossary

Advent: the first season of the church calendar and the beginning of the new year. It falls at the end of the normal calendar year and typically lasts most of the month of December. It is the season when we focus on the looming arrival of the newborn Jesus at Christmas.

Anthropic principle: term coined by Brandon Carter, the astrophysicist who noted that the universe looks as if it was always expecting life to emerge.

Baptism: the basic Christian rite of initiation into the church. The act of having water poured over one's head (or sometimes full immersion) is to symbolize our participation in the death of Jesus and resurrection of Jesus. You can be baptized as a child (in which case the parents and godparents make the vows for the baby and work hard to bring the child up in the faith) or as an adult.

Book of Common Prayer: the book used to organize the worship of The Episcopal Church. It goes back to Thomas Cranmer who produced the first Book of Common Prayer back in 1549. It has been revised many times since, and each area around the world where Anglicans worship has its own version.

Christmas: the birth of Jesus, which is marked by the church calendar in the Western church as December 25th and goes for twelve days of celebration.

Confirmation: the moment when a person takes on their baptismal vows for herself or himself. Typically the service of confirmation is preceded by confirmation classes, where a person learns about the faith.

Creeds: the statements of the Universal Church that describe our agreed-on understanding of doctrine (our beliefs).

Discipleship: the daily act of following Jesus through words and deeds as modeled and taught by Jesus in the Gospels.

Easter: marks the celebration of the resurrection of Jesus and runs for fifty days.

Epiphany: is both a celebration day and a season in the church year. It celebrates the coming of the magi to the infant Jesus each year on January 6, and the season celebrates the manifestation of Christ and ends the day before Ash Wednesday.

Eucharist: literally "grateful"; it is the term used to describe Holy Communion in The Episcopal Church. It is when the death of Jesus is remembered by the blessing of bread and wine.

Gospels: literally "good news"; the first four books of the New Testament—Matthew, Mark, Luke, and John. They tell the story about the life, death, and resurrection of Jesus.

Hellenistic: the culture of the Greeks, which heavily shaped the early church. This is the reason the New Testament is written in Greek, while the Old is written in Hebrew.

Incarnation: the Christian claim that God was in Jesus—uniquely present and disclosing the true nature of the Creator to the world.

Liturgy: literally the word means "the work of the people." It describes the structure, required responses, and order of the services. So in a Baptist Church, the structure can vary from week to week; in the liturgical traditions (e.g. Roman Catholic, Lutherans, and The Episcopal Church), the structure is set. In The Episcopal Church, the liturgy is found in the *Book of Common Prayer*.

Metaphysics: literally beyond physics. It is the study of the ultimate nature of everything that is; so it is the study of God, the origins of the universe, and areas such as life after death.

Neoplatonism: the tradition that is derived from Plato (c. 428 BCE–c. 348 BCE), one of the world's greatest philosophers. Plotinus (c. 204/5–270) is a neoplatonist philosopher who had a major impact on the early church.

Peace: the moment in the liturgy when the members of the congregation all greet each other and offer to each other "the peace of the Lord."

Pentecost: the coming of the Holy Spirit. The day itself is celebrated by the color red; the actual season is marked by green.

Postmodernism: the view held by some philosophers and theologians that we have moved beyond the modern period. Modernity is contrasted with the premodern (the period before the Enlightenment in the seventeenth century); and the postmodern period started in architecture in the late twentieth century and spread to other disciplines. Postmodern philosophers are deeply suspicious of definitive meanings and stress the complexity and approximate nature of truth.

Presiding bishop: the primate (the leading bishop) of The Episcopal Church. The presiding bishop is elected for a nine-year term at General Convention (which is the body that governs The Episcopal Church).

Priest: an ordained member of the clergy with the responsibility to provide the sacraments of the church to the people of God.

Rector: a title for the priest responsible for a parish (for the congregation).

Trinity: the Christian claim that God is properly understood as three persons in one; the three persons are traditionally called the Father, the Son, and the Holy Spirit. Theologians suggest that the symbol Father means source, origin, and is often associated with the creator; the symbol Son captures the revealing and redeeming aspect of God; and the Holy Spirit is the aspect of God that connects God with the world.

For Further Reading

Farwell, James W. *The Liturgy Explained*. Harrisburg: Morehouse Publishing, 2013. An accessible and thorough introduction to the liturgy of The Episcopal Church.

Hauerwas, Stanley. *Prayers Plainly Spoken*. Downers Grove, IL: InterVarsity Press, 1999. A great book for when finding words is challenging or accessible forms of prayer are desired.

Hawkins, Barney. *Episcopal Etiquette and Ethics: Living the Craft of Priesthood in the Episcopal Church*. Harrisburg: Morehouse Publishing, 2012. A good description of the Episcopal tribe and worldview, seen through the eyes of clergy.

Higton, Mike. *Difficult Gospel: The Theology of Rowan Williams*. New York: Church Publishing, 2004. Rowan Williams is probably the most thoughtful theological mind working in Anglicanism today. This is a gentle, delightful introduction to his theology.

Markham, Ian S. and Robertson, C.K. *Episcopal Questions, Episcopal Answers: Exploring Christian Faith*. New York: Morehouse Publishing 2014. Short succinct answers to all the major questions you might have about The Episcopal Church.

Markham, Ian S. *Liturgical Life Principles: How Episcopal Worship Can Lead to Healthy and Authentic Living*. New York: Morehouse Publishing, 2009. A journey through the liturgy of The Episcopal Church. The purpose is to help connect the liturgy with life.

Markham, Ian. S. *Understanding Christian Doctrine*. Oxford: Wiley Blackwell, 2008. This is intended as an accessible introduction to the major themes of the Christian faith—the nature of God, reasons for belief, the Trinity, the Incarnation, atonement, and life after death.

Placher, William C. *A History of Christian Theology: An Introduction*. Philadelphia: Westminster Press, 1983. This is a great survey of the early church and its foundations.

Stark, Rodney. *The Rise of Christianity: How the Obscure, Marginal Jesus Movement Became the Dominant Religious Force in the Western World in a Few Centuries*. San Francisco: Harper Collins, 1996. A sociologist provides a riveting analysis of why exactly the church grew so rapidly.

Webber, Christopher. *Welcome to The Episcopal Church: An Introduction to Its History, Faith, and Worship*. Harrisburg: Morehouse Publishing, 1999. This is an accurate and delightfully brief survey of the history and life of The Episcopal Church.

Wells, Samuel. *Be Not Afraid: Facing Fear with Faith*. Grand Rapids: Brazos Press, 2011. A delightful introduction to the spirit of Anglicanism.

Wells, Samuel. *What Episcopalians Believe: An Introduction*. Harrisburg: Morehouse Publishing, 2011. An excellent and accessible journey through the main beliefs of The Episcopal Church